# Vin Ordinaire

# Vin Ordinaire

## Poetry

## Terry Michael Hagans

CHB Media
Publisher

ISBN 9781946088871
LIBRARY OF CONGRESS CONTROL NUMBER: 2020902822

CHB MEDIA, PUBLISHER

(386) 690-9295

chbmedia@gmail.com


First Edition

Printed in the USA

Cover photography by cyano66

Illustration at page 8, from their 2016 calendar,
by permission of the brothers of Our Lady
of the Holy Cross Abbey.

I dedicate this volume to friends and acquaintances,
dead and living, unnamed here,
who, for many years, urged me to go beyond
one-on-one, face-to-face sharing of my poetry.
To publish it.

Foremost, I dedicate this work to the memory
of my late father, my late brother and my late mother.
My family.

*"The ultimate aim of a poet should be to touch our hearts by showing his own."*

– Philip Larkin

# CONTENTS

# Foreword

Not often have I had such a pleasant surprise in encountering the work of an unpublished poet.  Here is the voice of an astute observer of nature and of the human condition.  Terry Michael Hagans offers the reader an insightful retrospective of his own life experience via poems reflecting a wide range of emotions.  His poetry prompts us to exclaim: "Oh, I know that feeling!" as we experience his themes of joy, regret, loss and love. The poignancy of his verses is nicely balanced with touches of humor; Thierry, as I have come to address him, can laugh at himself in his sensitivity to human foibles.

When you begin to sip this poet's powerful and compelling *Vin Ordinaire*, do not think the title speaks of ordinary things.  On the contrary, this is a *dégustation extraordinaire*.

— John F. Foster

John Foster is a national poetry judge and an award-winning author of four poetry collections.  His latest publication, *A Gesture of Words – Poetry Forms and Formulas*, has earned the endorsement of Peter Meinke, former Poet Laureate of Florida.  Foster is noted for his poetry workshops for the Florida State Poets Association and for his entertaining readings for civic clubs throughout west-central Florida.  He is the founder and President of the Southshore Poets of Sun City Center.

# Preface

I was born in France of American parents, and was educated in the French school system. At age 11, I was enrolled for two years at the American School of Paris to learn, at a minimum, how to speak, to read, and to write in English. My family moved to the United States when I was 14. I attended Northeast High School in Fort Lauderdale ('67), and went on to graduate from Duke University with a B.A. in Philosophy ('71).

Several years later I began what would turn out to be a life as an investigator and mediator of labor-management disputes, and a commuter between Northern Virginia and Washington D.C. I became adept at drafting reports or decisions: descriptive, accurate, analytical, clear and thorough. My work had a pattern: listen, write.

When I decided to retire my identity as a labor relations professional, I understood that during my career I had fallen in love with language, in its oral delivery and in its written form. At some point silence took my hand and guided me: *listen to what you hear, write*! One by one pieces were born, and some now live in this book. If there is no title, it is only because none readily presented itself for publication; I let it go at that.

I am confident that much of what you are about to read is already written inside of you. We are cups filled with the same, common words. That is why I chose the title, *VIN ORDINAIRE*, literally ordinary wine, but better translated from the French as *TABLE WINE*. What is offered and available any day at a dinner table. Fancy this book as our table, at which one of us lifts a glass to say, *To your health, Santé*!

Terry Michael Hagans
Palm Coast, Florida

# Acknowledgements

This collection of poems or poetic pieces came together gradually through the help of certain persons who took an interest in my work. It is my pleasure to recognize them here.

In 2014 I learned that Michael Ray King, a local writer, hosted a monthly event in Flagler Beach, "The Inspired Mic". Each edition featured up to 16 authors of all stripes, and other artists, who were handed 6 minutes in which to show-case their gifts to a live audience. Each opportunity I received to recite my verses in that setting brought me closer to other verses asking to be written, and read. I began to imagine that one day I might collect them in a book. It was a virtuous cycle that peaked at Michael's May 2015 program when another guest, Stephanie Salkin, clued me in to the existence of the Florida State Poets Association.

This is not the place to name all the poets I went on to meet at poetry conventions whose published work speaks to me. But three have a place at this table. I was drawn to them in no small measure because of our matching humors, and because of our shared attachment to the French language.

John Foster welcomed with open arms my request that he review the manuscript for this book (it was my fortune, too, that then he happened to be free). He proceeded to study it for punctuation, syntax, spelling, grammar and clarity. He nudged me to rethink lines or words. We had copious exchanges, at times agreeing to disagree. His ardor challenged mine, and compelled me to take second looks at material he left untouched. The title "Found and Lost" was his instinctive response to my original "Lost and Found". He had sniffed out, for those who know him, a Fosterian alternative, proposing it in jest. I yielded to the obvious, a stand-alone rewrite.

Al Rocheleau and Dan Pels (and John no less) pushed me forward in good times and in bad, when I was cocksure and when I doubted. Each had his manner. Al prompted me to sort wheat from chaff, to attend to detail and syllable, to edit and edit, and to publish. He assured, and reassured me that what I write is poetry, that I am a poet. His influence and encouragement animate my writing today.

Dan's approach drew me out. He coaxed me to deliver at his Poetry Show, which he hosted at the time at wine bars in Volusia County, and I relished his offers to read to his audience his eccentric poetry, written in French. More than anything, Dan pressed me to write and write. I feel his presence in my poem "Guests and Visitors" and in the title I chose for this book. All told, Al and Dan drove me to the point of assembling the manuscript I would present to John.

I credit Charlie Greer for the title of this volume. Charlie, a gentleman from Louisville, Kentucky, is a former importer of French wines. He is also my friend and a tennis partner.  The original title for this book was *VIN ORDINAIRE* with the translation *TABLE WINE* appearing below it.  Charlie took issue with me while, of all things, we had a morning coffee.  The English cheapened or weakened the title, he thought. Well, that settled that.  It became *VIN ORDINAIRE*, alone.

Gary Broughman and CHB Media are the glue to this endeavor.  Gary is my publisher–Sherpa guide, without whom this volume would not be.  I am not competent to discuss the headaches he may have suffered, the challenges he mastered on my behalf.  But I know that we worked together quite effectively, and read each other very well.

Last and first, my wife, Carol, was steadfast, patient, and quiet (in the main) in suffering and supporting my efforts to bring this book, my first, to the light of day. Over the course of months, and months, and months. More, actually.

To each one I acknowledge above, my gratitude is far deeper than I can say.

# The Poems

## From My Heart To Yours

Here I am, your problem child,
the introverted Virgo poet.
I've come to write upon your face,
rest against your side,
sit and stand or walk with you,
meet your eyes,
hold your hand, touch its tips,
and when the time is right
behold, caress, abide upon your lips.

In its eighth life,
the cat turns jealous of the phoenix.

## Gifts

One night I met a light purer than any white I knew. Its love cribbled me ... through and through. I quivered, sat, It spoke – o, so brief this moment years ago. Love no man can give I'd met.

I followed Memory of the Light – or perhaps It guided me – on a path to a house of prayer. There, another night, lit and bright as a city cannot be, I stepped away into a forest clearing to see God's show. Toward light above from the warmth of dark below, I gazed into my new friend's twinkling, inviting glow. In quiet dear, peace secure, lost in breathless awe, I thought to speak, mustering instead simple words, whispered in slow, measured pace, "O ..., G --- O --- D! ... I ... LO ... V ... E ....... YOU!!!!!" A comet sailed by and fled from view.

Drink has different levels.
The one that's feared, known best of all,
is beyond giddiness and wanton lust.

But there is a fourth,
the mirth of Cana's Feast,
the one that monk and poet reach.

## Those Nights
## At Our Lady Of The Holy Cross Abbey

The moon and stars I see tonight
remind me of another time
when younger monks jogged and worked,
filled a country monastery that stilled my mind.

Those monks are dead or frail now.
But then and there
I met the moon and stars
and felt the passion of their Master's heart.

## Time

What is a clock
but something we make and watch?
On a visit to a friend's,
he led me through a room,
through doors he flung aside,
onto cultivated gardens, open air,
butterflies and bees,
scurrying furry beasts,
a stream, a fountain,
sounds not forming words,
while we stood or sat,
I don't recall,
before a sundial
neither one of us thought to read.

## Hosts

They vary.
One has unlocked doors through which you walk
meeting others and a meal,
while he turns his back to watch tv.

Another, his bell you ring,
are ushered in
onto a garden he loves to keep,
sipping wine until it's time to eat.

# New Year's Eve Tête-à-Tête

It appeared unexpectedly, like a thief,
shorn of desires felt a year or two ago.

There was no urge or need to call,
to wish, to hear a voice.
Those still to be found were music a week ago.
Their rings still dance, you see.

Our simple dinner tells it well, three tastes upon our plates,
bitter, bland and sweet,
what the New Year must usher in,
our destinies to greet.

Christmas is when we know winter's come,
sense the turn of spring once March is done.
Christmas is when we think of fall,
feel summer's passed.
Christmas comes and goes,
its gifts unwrapped,
a future now the past
recalled in later snows.

## To One Of My Best Friends


We visited tonight.
What a team we had been!
But some of your memories are lost on me.
Not all, far from it, could you but read me too,
dear tattered, weathered
Personal Telephone Address Directory.

To speak of moments is to court incoherent death.
A moment's not a moment, just a turn of speech,
a vain and slothful effort to share what can't be owned.

Speak of an event if you must,
of a prom, a wedding, a World Cup,
something months await.
It will be written on a page and more,
the obituary waiting to be born.
But moments, all of them,
are what you breathe and cannot replicate.

## Dining At Home Is A Better Deal

Tucked into an almost-cozy corner,
capping off a frenzied day at an evening tavern table,
the sun was setting in the bay
while, around your friends and you,
rambling screens, scripts and scenes rumbled on.
Discussions turned to this or that.
Ice cubes tumbled on the floor two tables down —
the smiling, puzzled waitress had missed her mark.
Dinners were ferried out.
Rising, blaring speakers, mumbles
fed upon themselves,
carrying grunts and snorts and laughs.
Images came and went, a zoo, a trough,
audience mixed with actors,
some practiced, others not.
The cost of admission, including a flirt or smirk,
was settled once dessert, coffee, another wine,
drew applause or a sideways nod.

Rising, noticed or unnoticed,
straightening without a bow
to a prepared, perhaps sincere *Please come again*,
you walk off stage, out of the giant screen,
onto the street below, leaving behind your role
in an animated comic or tragic strip
of families, flappers, flappy gadabouts,
and others without name,
hanging out on this bustling, lantern-lit, noisy stage,
eager to sate or numb their senses for a price
through words found only on a menu
in a replica of Plato's Cave.

# Flutters

The excitement of the party atmosphere!
Pillar candles wave their flames
about the small-town square.
People mill around or mix.
Groups of twos or threes become fours,
disband, root, disperse
atop its cobblestones.
Tables wobble at the slightest touch.

Shadowed eyes glance,
almost unperceived,
throughout the walled, fenced-in nook
into other peering, furtive looks,
dissipated, dissolute,
cocktail-tinted flickers painting others' masks;
fingers, palms alert to steady drinks,
or greet at last the face
they had come to meet.

*Is this how loneliness feeds itself,*
asked my solitude.
*Let's discuss that tomorrow*, I replied,
*when you and I alone are in each other's company,*
*loneliness nowhere for us to see.*

## Restraint

I see your beauty and your grace
through filmy eyes, child aged,
speak as best I can,
disorderly,
while you enjoy, laugh and touch.

I wish it could be more,
I wish we had more time
though when all is said and done,
it's right just as it is,
incomplete, unfulfilled
yet wholly without stain,
no matter all the looks and touch,
all we'd wish to gain.

## Shuffles

It's snowing.
You undress.
It's dark.

It's snowing.
You undress the dark.

They said he was a poet, put him in that box.
They said he showed much promise,
urged him to find his form.
And when he found his space,
they frowned upon his words,
the ones he'd nurtured all his life.
He paced about his window,
his mind a raging storm,
when Alice and The Little Prince led him through a wall
to meet Teddy Bear and Ragged Ann chatting over tea.

## Today

Memory, dear and constant friend,
I have this funny thing to say.
A picture reminded me of my younger days,
another of where I am today.
Naturally, I thought of what was in between –
o, there are snapshots, running themes,
deeply dear and so and so –
but none of them so clear
as youthful innocence
calling me back to stay.

## A Fool's Mystery

Photographs, castles in the sand,
are story books for hungry looks
imagining what they cannot know,
themselves storybooks
with nothing new to show.

How are you, Terry? I'll
be retiring next June after
37 years at UNC. Isn't it
incredible? I feel like I

May the joy
and peace of Christmas
be with you now
and through the new year.

am a fifteen year old!

Federico Gil

## Christmas Time

Christmas cards,
if you remember,
weren't just greetings, wishful tidings,
but memories kindled once again
when you wrote them,
and found names
no longer able
to hear your voice or read your pen.

## My Buddy

He was my boss and friend,
a wrecking ball, a golden heart.
I'd spent my life for him,
unaware time would run her course.
Aging, he retired, we parted ways,
stayed in touch by heart
more than anything.
I never saw the shadow he became,
the frail bull they drugged.
He's dead today as he was yesterday.
Tonight I thought of him.

## Loyal Friends

That cloudy sky,
its swath of rolling gray,
an old friend dropping in,
saying *Hi*.
The wind and waves reaching shore,
always new,
old friends all the same.
The blueness of the sky,
the blinding naked sun,
another friend, another day.
How few these passing friends,
so fresh their tones and tunes,
in dress never shown again.

## Found And Lost

Rain, long-time friend,
buried in my skin,
I know your many sounds.

But your pinging on a roof,
above an open door,
plays a music I know not how to type.

### 9/29 Archangels' Day

How funny, strange what we think or feel.
We smell something sweet,
Christmas cookies or a tree ...
see adored ornaments
while others just won't do.
A taste perhaps just came through,
one of those we loved the most,
a gentle touch,
just enough
to see a face pass through a door
hosting or visiting, sitting down to pour.

## Anne

We met one spring riding bikes.
She went to another school, had brown hair,
wore soft, seamed leather loafers without socks,
notches lighter than her tan.
She spoke to me.

We met again.  Was it the next morning?
At the same spot, just around the block?
She pointed out her family's house.
I got lost, shyly sighed, my words in disarray.

Years flew by, they flew away.

I thought of her an autumn day, lucked out,
found her trace.  Her name I'd not forgot.
Alum deceased, the high school said.
The sigh that came had nothing it could say.

## Before The Moon Rose Unseen
## On A Cloudy Night


I saw your face at dusk
around or in the ocean's calm, smooth sound
washing onto sand.
The sun has set,
a bird or two dive in
for dinner or a snack.
It's quiet.  The dazzling red behind my back
is now a fading pink,
the ocean gray as far as eye can see,
the color of the slate on which your name is set,
away from here,
there in Georgia where you sleep.

## A Hallowed Place

I never gave you roses,
it hadn't crossed my mind.
Had we met again another time
I'd have chosen red,
but knowing now we cannot meet
I had to think a bit
and felt that short of red,
you'd like yellow, white
and sent them through my mind,
on this cruel date you died,
to find you anyway.

## The Bookcase

Trinkets and monuments,
stones, shells and wood found along the way,
embellish and adorn
a crowded cozy space,
clones of magic clover leaves
picked years before
from fields and lawns in child's play.

## Transfigured

The market's opening up again;
it's Friday morning at the beach.
Farmers, vendors, sort, display
tented goods and wares.
One by one customers appear,
trace of night folded into dawn.
A hollered *Hi* snubbed its calm,
the startled cyclist waving back
her dreamy stare.

Later on, bread broken, wine in hand,
garlic flavors meeting night,
the morning's panoply of mimes returned as cinema,
a dance, an instrumental balm,
matins' still-life scenes
become a minstrel's vespers psalm.

## My Thoughts Are Not Your Thoughts

– Isaiah 55:8

O, kind snow, thought the tiny twig,
coat me to be noticed and stand out.
Fall she did from the cloud,
coating one and all,
little twig and every limb.
They all looked beautiful
and all stood out.

The tumbling crests called me from my room
into the darkness of the night
to linger at my feet, to mourn them at the shore,
vanquished each in turn upon the clever beach.

A bird flew by, to and fro, no higher than my head,
letting out peculiar shrieks.
It may have been the sandpiper I would later follow
under shifting pellet rain,
stepping in, rushing back, pecking every chance he had,
both of us spellbound
each time the ocean vanished in the sand.

## Vacations

Summer but a week away,
dawn off to another place,
the sand began to bake
and a certain busyness overtook our porch.
Voices on the walk, a mower on the lawn,
a copter in the air, a motor in the street.

Waves stole upon the beach
while cities on the sea coasted into port,
azure sky under threat from swift, huffy clouds.
A bathing pelican took off,
a bird – what kind? – landed on the rail with a shriek,
and was gone. I didn't see it flee.
Beading sweat ran off my hand
to blur the ink that found this page,
the noise of my thought.
I put away the pen.

To behold a kaleidoscope of butterflies
or another set of eyes,
instantly luminous or opaque,
is the voyage and vacation
I much prefer to take.

## Reverie

There's something about the beach when no one is around.
Like early morning in a city, or any quiet dawn.

The ocean's passion brushes trackless sand,
invites you for a walk,
because you're married, because you're not,
as your eyes and ears hold her waves
while she kisses and perfumes your shyness and your gaze.

## To My American Friend

Now that you've seen Honfleur and Giverny
you may spot their trace in me,
fathom why my tennis strokes
come across as lines of poetry.

## Don't Ask Me About My Loves

Sometimes you think you've got it
and then you're jammed,
bottled up.
The strokes don't flow,
the ball won't clear the net,
finds it yet again,
and you can't explain
nor clearly write it
and struggle to remember
just how to spell
PATETIC.

## Brevity Is Clarity

The look is there,
the kiss is next.
In best of worlds
there is no text.

## A Minuet

Let me meet you early,
let us not be late.
Choose the time,
name the place.
I will meet you there
to dance our minutes
face to face.
I will meet you very early.
You can call it late.

# Hello

You say goodbye,
peck her cheek;
she kisses half your lips.
You remember,
and when you see her later,
ask, *Do you mind*,
kiss her on her lips.
*It's been a long time*,
you let out.
*Yes, a long time*, she replies.

# Eden

*Oh you can't go back to Kansas*
*It just up and blew away* – John Stewart


I asked her to remove her robe.
It slipped off, she waded in
lofting giggles, laughs,
quiet most of all.
We barely touched,
felt water wash away our skins.
We were young again, children without masks,
our parents very near
calling us back in.
But how could we?
Our robes had upped and blown away.

## Bon Appétit

There are two kinds of snail shells:
the one in which they put the snail,
the one in which the snail hides,
nibbled lettuce at each one's side.

## Not Made In Heaven

Have you, have you ever wondered
whether a flea prefers a dog
over that other whiskered pet?
When you do, consider this.
Fleas, I'm told, live to hop
whereas a cat prefers to nap.

## The Prodigal

Were you a salmon in a can,
poetry your opening to light,
would you gasp, *Oh, no, not air again,*
or ponder where these lines might bend?

**?**

*I met the deadline!*
she explained with glee.
Off to the side, I pondered
the kind of person she might be.

# The Literalist

*in memory of a dear friend,*
*and of her clear voice*


*Mercy*, said she.
Off I went to look it up.
I found the Aral and the Med.
One named Black, another Red.
But for Mur there was no Sea.

I reported back, sad though proud,
explaining Mur is not a sea,
only to be veiled in another cloud
when she turned aside and thought,
with a smile and a sigh,
*Oh my, dear me!*

Aren't we prehistoric to some degree,
amoeba-like in sensitivity,
coiling, shying from stimuli,
Venus fly-traps possibly?

# A Rude Awakening

It studied me quizzically,
the parakeet in its cage.

*Bizet*, I asked,
*do you think* ... I went on for quite a while.
Bizet nodded on and off,
never squawked nor peeped,
all signs that he agreed or was inclined.

Yes, inclined he was,
lending me his ear,
but so inclined that he fell off his perch,
plopping on his papered floor, rigid as a corpse.
I stood alarmed and scared.

His owner turned her head and chided him.
*Bizet, you naughty little bird,*
and he fluffed a feather as he caught his breath.

*Don't be concerned*, she grinned,
*Bizet nods off when he's bored to death!*

## Guests And Visitors

For the most part they seem happy –
another batch of visitors
has come to learn and have some fun.

A roar just came from over there
and it got the rooster crowing
while hyenas laughed it off,
and the seals barked, *Give us more!*,
clapping, clapping, *Encore, Encore!!*,
animating the monkey house
into gestures not fit to print.

Only the gorilla seemed sad,
and the bear was absent from his lair –
two mysteries a stork gone mad
ponders quietly, as it struts
back and forth in its own cage.

And the people come and go,
and the people come and go,
and the giraffes taunt the elephants
while the tiger has escaped.

## Unmoored

Her mast and furled sails
streamed by without a stutter,
homeward bound this early spring,
memories crated, packed.
A figure aft watching petals from her hand
fall one by one
into the disappearing wake.

## Looking Back

Looking back on it,
52 years ago,
my life as I'd known it
came to a sudden end.
It took a turn,
not because I'd turned 14,
but because my father died
and we had to move away,
move away from the place,
the place that never went away.

## A Familiar Sound

I heard a chugging train and its familiar horn
pass by my favorite brook.
I did not move, cocked my head
to better hear its say.

How strange, I realized.
This train that's followed me for years
had been telling me all along:
*It's okay, I'm rolling on,*
*it's time for you to find your way.*

## We're Modern, Ya Know

To say our world's modern
is a trick we pull upon ourselves.
Some things are modern.
Japan's 300-mile per hour magnetic train,
robotic restaurant reservations.

It's better though, I think,
to say our world is what it can only be:
contemporary,
as in contemporary furniture,
contemporary notions.

## Soliloquy

How can one know if there's a God?
I heard crickets and frogs tonight.

Who is I?
I, I, sometimes you, you,
we or they,
ever coming from willing, willful eyes.
I's who know more than God.
The I who can't create itself
(himself, herself, to please another set of I's).
The I who couldn't spawn a cricket or a frog.
The I who makes cars and aeroplanes.
The I who flies to Mars,
becomes a mob.

We're portraits on a wall, neatly tucked within a frame,
desperate for a mirror we cannot find.
Portraits in a frame see a lot, don't they?
But do they feel, hear and touch,
and has man or she created such?

Why talk?
Out of fear silence is too much,
to impress or woo,
to break the ice, meet someone new,
hear ourselves again,
force ourselves, our points of view?
Why say *Look at this*
when a certain silence reigns,
why not wait 'til dinner's set,
the breaking of the bread?

Why not write?
It, too, is a tango thing —
a quiet thing
that speaks and plants a kiss
one can later taste and read again.

I'd once fancied turning Bach's chords into words.
I loved Beethoven, Rameau, Baudelaire, too.
They all said something new.  Yet, only the Psalms
clearly spoke the truths my silence knew.
My pen was fine, sense of beauty fair, longings known.
But I've little left to say, my pen is very dry,
now that friends have died, our dreams no longer clay.

## Alma Mater

Our Gothic walls,
thick and mute,
held us in their care.
They were never meant to speak
but to be a code we learned,
the language we would seek.
The stories we can tell,
the stories we have told,
about our time within those walls,
the walls of other hearts
who'd also heard their calls.

## GDI's
### 1967 - 1971

When rush time came at college,
some of us didn't pledge.
We gave ourselves an English name,
actually American,
in response to their dubbing us da Latins
which, if Greekified, would have been
Gamma Delta Iota.
I became a Catholic after those glorious days
and it pains me now to some degree
to recall what GD meant.
But Iota I am proud to say stood for
Independent.

## East Campus, Duke University
## January 1969

We walked a mile or more
to the store,
bringing back our wine
that snowy night
to sip and drink
up in that magnolia tree,
sharing everything we felt
until we were dearly numb.

It took years before we met again,
to share the little left to say,
that carefree, careless night
resiliently unrepeatable
still within our sight.

# Tapestry

A fish flapping in a dripping net,
gasping in thinning air.
A stunned deer stopping in its tracks
sporting a silent querying stare.
Images of whom we often are,
in two places all at once,
driving somewhere with a stranger or a friend,
standing, drink in hand, at some event,
floating off into ourselves
to meet frisky otters in a pond,
busy squirrels in the fall,
thoughts and scenes off point
to all the conversations going on.

## Yes, I Know ...

All I'm saying
is I don't like it.
Yes, I saw your body
lying cold.
Yes, I know you left.
Yes, I know they turned you into ash.
Yes, I know ...
I know your voice is gone
your wit will never come again.
I know all that
don't you see?

Yes, I know ...

# The Goodbye Bottle

We used to jump on the express
slowly finding, one by one, the local,
never knowing which we liked the best.

We loved our books and articles,
magazines, periodicals,
desks and coffee tables,
glasses full of wine or scotch,
water by the side.

We knew better than to share our hearts too often.
Irreverence and comedy made more sense,
though sometimes pressures built, and then
a call or visit beckoned.
We were impractical complements.

We knew goodbye is served just once,
took a chance, aged it well,
until you called one day to say
you had raised it from the cellar.
It stood between us several days,
becoming brilliant, becoming clear,
before we let it breathe.
No goodbye poured out,
just a flourish worth the wait.

I left you there, at the station,
learning the next morning
you had reached your final destination.
I searched our empty bottle,
its sediment wholly settled,
its glass brilliant, clear.

And, at last, the word spilled out.

## Your Stony Effigy

Damn it,
you always knew how to keep a secret.
You'd held court one more time, last night,
sent us off, and when we met again,
your pain and thirst had become
body on a hospice bed at clammy noble rest,
effigy without a parting qualm.

## Reflections

Tomorrow is trash, recycle and tennis day,
no rain foreseen,
our last week gone,
I, back home.

I'd never taken out the trash
thinking about your visits and your stays,
our fun and play,
nor dragged you grumbling to the courts
under early morning sun.
But tomorrow I may carry you in my heart.
Everything is changed
now that you rest in Georgia clay.

# A Storm Reined In

Ah, the mail that came today!
When it rains, it pours.
Feast or famine, the adages go on.
Days go by when mail of a certain sort never comes.
Today was not that kind.

Jokes, information, pleas and thank you's flooded in.
Can you play tennis Saturday, asked one.
From a town three hours' drive away, a friend's wife,
writing from his station,
announced he'd been up all night,
could not eat or drink,
hospice would now come in.

No voices spoke, other e-mails trailed in,
and I wrote back I'd like to play, come Saturday.


It was our first visit since December to their "little bit of Heaven", words on a wooden sign in their outdoor living area, their patio and garden. All afternoon a dark August sky lurked, crept in, but its fury never raged. It released nothing more than one crisp lightning bolt bridging air and earth, followed by a delayed companion rumble, the closing act, yielding the stage to a sunny early evening and a gentle rain, itself become a drizzle.

While they prepared dinner, I had stepped outside to be alone, to capture what I could of the new, open garden so unlike the cloistered haven he had established around their kidney-shaped swimming pool at their previous home in Coral Springs, southeast of here. I couldn't count the mornings, afternoons, evenings, nights spent in its unaffected lush privacy, elegance inviting liberties.

Invited, the past swept in, welled, elusive as the present before which I stood, stone boundaries, pavers, a banana tree, pineapples, papayas, a mix of flowers, gnomes, lights awaiting guests, a work in progress nearly done. It was quiet, almost empty, except for some chirps, a distant hum of cars, bursts of kitchen laughter from Gwen and Carol, and laggard trickles playing notes in the downspout next to me, unexpected triggers to questions it was too late to ask because they belonged to December when we'd last seen Gwen at Spencer's memorial service. I recalled the history of his illness, our discussions when he still could talk, his resignations, hopes, our last face to face, our final chat. An emptiness covered me until the call for dinner came.

Gwen would die just short of two years later.

## To My Oldest New World Friend

We know you're dying,
cannot talk as you once did.
I feel a lot, have few words.
What would you say were you standing in my shoes?
Would you say anything,
would you ache, would you pine?
Would you look to our high school days,
what happened later on?
Would we talk about our latest finds?

And when we say goodbye,
the last thing on our minds,
would you be brave and show your eyes?

## It Is What It Is

It is what it is, a favorite tune of yours over the years.
It was one thing to feel you'd soon be gone,
another to see firsthand
only a miracle could reverse the course.
Your wit's still there
in your weariness,
not so quick but there.
You've made your peace,
touched and sorted through your past,
take some pills, stay warm
in the one seat that fits your form more or less,
everyday a little less.

## In The Echoes Of My Mind

Mucus in your lungs,
slowly spoken throaty words,
gurgling coughs rushing up,
mockingbirds of ocean waves.
Listening to my words, my voice no rest,
welcomed excitement mounted in your veins
vainly trying to be still.
I'd no thought the call I placed would lead to this.
A message left.  Your spouse's voice perhaps,
not yours, not now in the middle of an eve.
You could have let it go – you must have been alone –
but you saw who called, had to answer,
say hello, bid goodbye.
That was it, wasn't it?
The nebulizer you chased struggling from our talk
will only do so much.
Our chat was very brief.  I'm glad you took the call.

What happened?
Neither thinning air nor friend could say.
It was his question, just thrown out.
Something happened, something changed,
once cold now he's hot.
Hospice brought in a bed,
a very busy day.
Tonight his tired wife
sits alone by his side,
hoping, praying, memories binding,
drifting into his hidden sleep,
mindful tomorrow is not another day.

"The soul that is quick to turn to speaking and conversing is slow to turn to God."

— St. John of the Cross

## Letting Go

The phone rings
until your recorded voice announces
no one is available.
Anyhow, your wife returned my call,
saying she'd been away,
with the children, and so and so ...
I wasn't home.  So, I tried again,
and left more words,
prompted by your own.
I wish you could explain what's going on.
She used to take my calls, speaking, I imagine,
from your gorgeous garden window,
your stricken wife and widow.

## A Tale of Two Lives

I told you of the robin who for two days
pecked around each morning,
and of the butterfly I'd followed,
while you recalled being trapped for hours
in your elevator the day before a cruise to Europe
and talked of other distant space.

## Artistic Sympathy

We were artists
capturing each other's glance,

I, paused, sitting at a table
in view of her passing, photographic eyes
carrying some of me away
each time she curled by,

wondering who she was
until her name appeared on the bill
and she took my pen to write it out
in her native script,

her chartreuse Macedonian eyes
asking mine how well I understood
the language I did not speak,
the private moments snared and shaped
between a customer and his waitress
clad in formal black and white.

*se.rein', n. Meteorol.*

A mist or very fine rain, which sometimes falls
from a clear sky a few moments after sunset.

### *Eternity*

He who binds to himself a joy
Does the winged life destroy;
He who kisses the joy as it flies
Lives in eternity's sunrise.

– William Blake

# Study Of A Store Clerk

I cannot see your face,
know not who you are.
I wonder what you think,
wonder where you are.

But questions miss the mark.
You're a special case,
a mist of pregnant pauses,
a sea of guarded clefs,
writ across your pianist's hands,
your smooth and gliding gait.

You are the seasons of the year,
serein upon a bay, a litany of tides,
a tended garden, potted clay,
countless hues of dew and dappled shade.

You are breath, a breeze,
dawn throughout the day,
the moon at noon,
star-lit sky in darkest night,
a shooting star by lucky sight,
a welling tear in Blake's "Eternity".

You spoke this unaware
as you swept across the floor,
from behind your counter space,
toward something hidden, on display,
in a dream I had while wide awake,
oh lovely, haunting, hound of grace.

## That Silly Sadness

It felt silly,
so childlike,
to feel sad when you said good-bye
to your brother or to your mother
because it was time for you to go back home,
miles and miles away.
Oddly odd to feel the same
toward old friends
when their visits came to end.
You vowed to rise above it.

But comes the day when good-byes disappear.
In vain you wish for a call or letter
and the promise of a trip
because now you want to say good-bye,
to feel that silly sadness,
mindful you never rose above it.

Memory is a funny child.
She's a photograph,
photographed again and again,
a harpoon that freezes time.

Memory changes colors,
is not one point in time.
Forgive her, then, all the more today,
lest she seize you for herself
in a grave and callous way.

## Imprints Never Die

People die, places die,
professors, friends, family,
watering holes, ways of life.
Or perhaps we run away.

Yet, images never leave, imprints never die.
They travel with us
toward our moment beyond time and space,
horizon gone without a trace.

This page is a moment,
something frozen.
Call it a painting, a photograph.
It aspires to the timeless
which only the drowning know
as they surrender, their farewell hidden,
private,
a good-bye lacking tears.
There is no ETA or ETD,
no ticket gate, no walk onto a quai,
no backside seen,
only perhaps one last wave
much like the tree that falls
when no one hears its sound.

# Postscript

# A POSTSCRIPT TO VIN ORDINAIRE

THREE WRITERS BESIDES JOHN FOSTER HAVE penned warm sentiments for *VIN ORDINAIRE*. I thank them for giving their time to read its manuscript and for choosing to comment. Their full expressions appear below (excerpts line the back-cover).

"I would ask readers to stop awhile, as I have, to sip these poems as though the poet has offered you a glass of everyday table wine which is a delightful treat. Terry Hagans' ponderings flow with dancing moments, reflective pauses, hearty hellos and poignant farewells. They touch the reader with a familiarity that lingers."

— Janet Watson, Award-winning poet
and author of *Eyes Open, Listening*

Janet Watson is a former journalist who has morphed into poet. Her poems consistently win awards and find publication in anthologies and literary journals. She has written several chapbooks and published a book-length collection of her poems. She is president of New River Poets, and for nine years she chaired a statewide Student Poetry Contest for the Florida State Poets Association. Her current literary project is a historic novel for young readers.

"A Janus paradox of friend and stranger turns on time, space, courts the intimacy of meals and conversation, revels in importance of the comic insignificance of things and the wisdom of love, pent in a heretofore unrecorded philosopher who has woven his treatise out of air in every thought between breaths ... now puts it to paper, coming home in the poems of this book.  Part Rimbaud, part Pascal, part émigré-savant, Terry Hagans paints the interior of mind and heart."

— Al Rocheleau

Al Rocheleau, President, Florida State Poets Association; Founder, Twelve Chairs Advanced Poetry Course; Recipient, Thomas Burnett Swann Award; Nominee, Forward Poetry Prize (U.K.); Author, *On Writing Poetry* (2010); *Falling River: Collected Poems 1976-2016* (2017).

"Michel, as I have called him since we met, is an amazing poet who allows the reader to feel the sensitive emotions that he brings to each page. With vivid images and heartfelt language, Michel Hagans brings you inside his world of experiences. *Vin Ordinaire* is far from being ordinary.  It is "top-shelf" premium wine in a book.  It is a poetry book to be hugged close to one's heart and cherished as one would cherish a special friend."

— Dan Pels

Dan Pels is a native Parisian, a bilingual poet, and a surrealist author of six poetry books. He has a Master's Degree in French Literature from Syracuse University. He has performed at the Dali Museum in St. Petersburg, Florida and encourages poets by co-hosting and producing the Poetry Show at the HUB in New Smyrna Beach, Florida.